RUTHERFORD B. *Hayes*

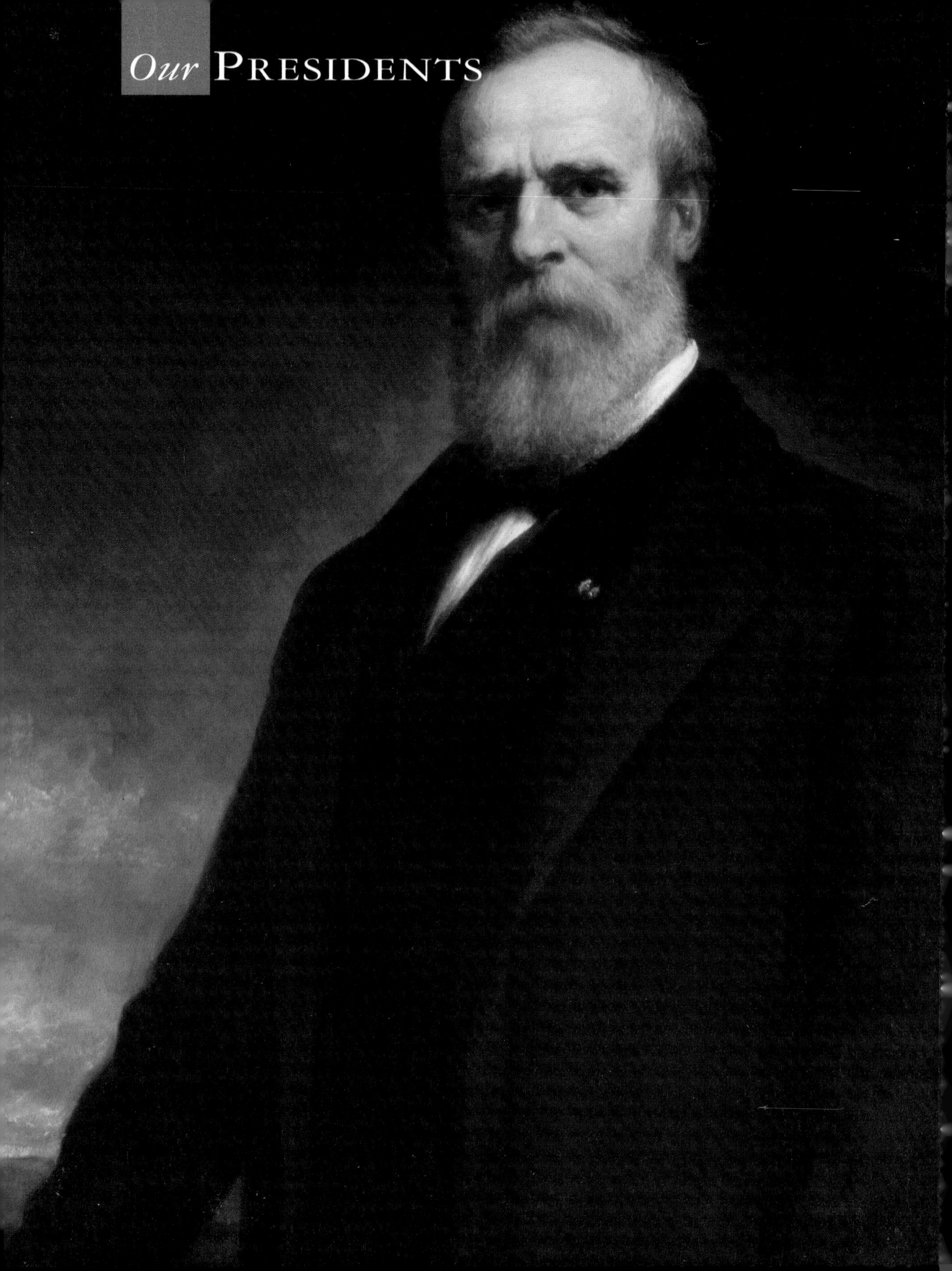

RUTHERFORD B. *Hayes*

OUR NINETEENTH PRESIDENT

By Sandra Francis

SPIRIT
of America™

The Child's World®, Inc.
Chanhassen, Minnesota

6

RUTHERFORD B. *Hayes*

Published in the United States of America by The Child's World®, Inc.
PO Box 326 • Chanhassen, MN 55317-0326 • 800-599-READ • www.childsworld.com

Acknowledgments
The Creative Spark: Mary Francis-DeMarois, Project Director; Elizabeth Sirimarco Budd, Series Editor; Robert Court, Design and Art Direction; Janine Graham, Page Layout; Jennifer Moyers, Production

The Child's World®, Inc.: Mary Berendes, Publishing Director; Red Line Editorial, Fact Research; Cindy Klingel, Curriculum Advisor; Robert Noyed, Historical Advisor

Photos
Cover: White House Collection, courtesy White House Historical Association; Bettmann/Corbis: 12; ©Corbis: 15, 18, 26; Collections of the Library of Congress: 11, 14, 21, 22, 23, 29, 31; Rutherford B. Hayes Presidential Center, Fremont, OH: 6, 7, 8, 9, 10, 12, 16, 19, 20, 25, 28, 33, 35; Stock Montage: 27

Library of Congress Cataloging-in-Publication Data
Francis, Sandra.
    Rutherford B. Hayes : our nineteenth president / by Sandra Francis.
        p. cm.
    ISBN 1-56766-856-9 (alk. paper)
    1. Hayes, Rutherford Birchard, 1822–1893—Juvenile literature. 2. Presidents—United States—Biography—Juvenile literature. [1. Hayes, Rutherford Birchard, 1822–1893. 2. Presidents.] I. Title
    E682 .F73 2001
    973.8'3'092—dc21

                                                    00-010645

11   21   33

Contents

Chapter ONE

A Devoted Family

Rutherford Hayes was an honest, hardworking gentleman who believed in always doing what was right. He became the 19th president in 1877.

FIVE YEARS BEFORE RUTHERFORD BIRCHARD Hayes was born, his parents moved their family from Vermont to the town of Delaware, Ohio. Mrs. Hayes's younger brother, Sardis Birchard, went with them. Mr. Hayes bought a business, rented farmland, and built the first brick house in town. Life in Ohio was happy and successful for the Hayes family. Unfortunately, in July of 1822, Mr. Hayes became seriously ill. He died soon after.

Rutherford was born on October 4, 1822, about three months after his father's death. His Uncle Sardis became the devoted guardian of the Hayes family. He was like a father to newborn Rutherford and his brother and sister, Lorenzo and Fanny. Sardis Birchard worked hard and soon became a successful banker.

He was able to take good care of the family.

Ruddy, as Rutherford's family called him, was a fragile and sickly child. His mother was determined to help him get better. Her devotion to Ruddy grew even stronger when tragedy struck the family again. Lorenzo, who was just nine years old, drowned while ice-

skating. Fanny was now Ruddy's only playmate, but her sense of adventure and her love of poetry made her a good companion. The two children enjoyed playing outdoors. In wintertime, they spent their days reading. Ruddy was still too ill to attend school, but Mrs. Hayes wanted him to be ready when he was well. She taught him to read and write.

As Ruddy's health and strength improved, he was finally able to go to school. Uncle Sardis took an interest in his education.

Rutherford's father died just before he was born, so the future president was raised by his mother, Sophia Birchard Hayes, shown above.

Interesting Facts

▶ Hayes was born at his parent's home in Ohio. The doctor's fee for the delivery was $3.50.

7

Hayes's uncle, Sardis Birchard, stepped in to help raise the Hayes children. He was a successful businessman who took good care of his sister's family.

He sent 14-year-old Ruddy to private school, where he prepared for college. Two years later, Ruddy enrolled at Kenyon College in Gambier, Ohio. His teachers and classmates admired him. He was not only an excellent student, but a gentleman as well. He graduated in 1842 at the top of his class.

Rutherford kept a diary from the time he was 12 until his death at age 70. As a young man, he wrote about his goals in this journal. "I am determined to acquire a character **distinguished** for energy, firmness, and **perseverance,**" he vowed. He also wrote that he hoped to be known as an honest man. He would work to live up to these goals throughout his life.

While Rutherford pursued his education, Fanny met and married William Platt. She and her mother moved to Platt's home in Columbus, Ohio. Rutherford spent a year living with them after he graduated from college. By this time, Rutherford had decided to become a lawyer. He studied law, German, and French. He also worked in an office to gain experience. But Rutherford knew he would have limited opportunities in Columbus. He decided to enroll at Harvard Law School, one of the best schools in the country. In 1845, he received his law degree. He began to work at a law office in Lower Sandusky, Ohio. (Lower Sandusky would soon be renamed Fremont.)

Rutherford moved to Cincinnati in 1849. There he set up his own a law office. He also joined clubs where he met Cincinnati's most powerful men. Rutherford became known for his honesty and skill as a lawyer. He was active in local **politics** and later joined the **Republican Party,** one of the **political parties** of the day.

As his career blossomed, Rutherford began to think of marriage. Back in 1847, he had met a young girl named Lucy Webb. Lucy was only 16 years old at the time, and

As a young lawyer, Hayes became known in Cincinnati as a good man and a successful lawyer. Soon members of the Republican Party would encourage him to enter politics.

Mr. and Mrs. Hayes had their first child in 1853. They named him Sardis, in honor of Rutherford's uncle. On the day of his son's birth, Rutherford wrote the following in his diary: "November 6, 1853— On Friday, the 4th, at 2 PM, Lucy gave birth to our first child—a son. I hoped … that the little one would be a boy. How I love Lucy, the mother of my boy!"

Rutherford had little interest in her. Years later, he remembered first meeting the "bright, sunny-hearted little girl not quite old enough to fall in love with." But when Lucy was a college student, they met again. He was taken by her beauty and intelligence. "I feel that you will not only be the making of my happiness," he wrote to her, "but also of my fortunes or success in life." In his own diary, Rutherford described Lucy's "low sweet voice" and "soft rich eyes." Finally, he penned the words, "By George! I am in love with her!"

At age 18, Lucy graduated from Wesleyan Female College in Cincinnati. She and Rutherford became engaged and then married at her parents' home in December of 1852. She was 21 years old, and Rutherford was 30. Marriage to Lucy had a positive effect on Rutherford's career. She was a kind and intelligent person who cared about people. One day, he wrote a tribute to Lucy in his diary: "A better wife I never hoped to have."

HAYES ALWAYS BELIEVED SLAVERY WAS WRONG, ALTHOUGH HE DID NOT speak out against it as a young man. When he married Lucy Webb, he became much more firmly opposed to it. He even used his skills as a lawyer to defend runaway slaves in court. Lucy told her husband a story that made him think hard about the evils of slavery. While away on business, her father **inherited** some slaves. Mr. Webb could not bear the thought of owning another human being. He quickly returned to his home, planning to set the slaves free.

Before he was able to free them, Mr. Webb became very sick and died. This left Lucy's mother with three small children and little money. People said that she could sell the slaves and live comfortably. To this suggestion, Mrs. Webb replied, "Before I will sell a slave, I will take in washing to support my family." Soon after, the slaves were set free.

11

Chapter TWO

The War Years

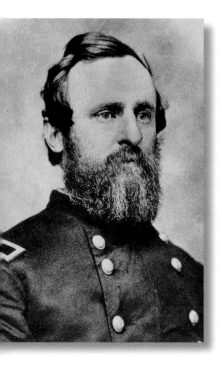

Rutherford Hayes had a distinguished military career. By the end of the Civil War, he had reached the rank of major general.

FOR MANY YEARS, THE ISSUE OF SLAVERY HAD been tearing the nation apart. More and more people in the northern states were opposed to it. But Southerners refused to give up their slaves. They were sure they could never run their large farms, called plantations, without the free labor the slaves provided. By the early 1860s, it appeared that the country could not avoid a **civil war.**

Rutherford Hayes listened with interest to the disagreements between the North and the South. By 1861, 11 Southern states had **seceded** from the **Union** to form their own country. They called it the **Confederate** States of America. On April 12, 1861, the Confederates fired on Union soldiers at Fort Sumter, and the American Civil War began.

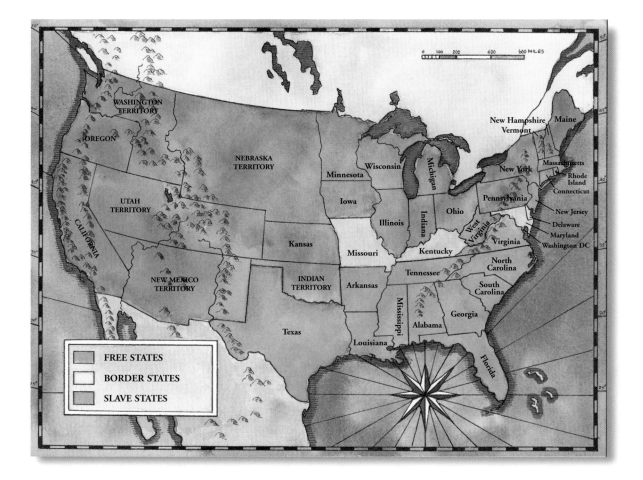

President Lincoln made an urgent request for 75,000 volunteers to join the Union army. Hayes joined the Burnet Rifles, a group of volunteer soldiers in Cincinnati. In June, the Ohio governor made Hayes a major in the 23rd Ohio Volunteer **Regiment.** Hayes promised to serve in the army for three years, thinking the war would end in just a few months. Unfortunately, this was not to be. Hayes would dedicate himself to winning the war for the next four years.

In 1861, most slave states seceded from the Union to form the Confederate States of America. But four slave states decided to fight with the Union. These were called the border states because they sat on the border between the North and the South. President Lincoln and other leaders did not outlaw slavery in these states because the Union needed their support.

13

The Confederate attack on Fort Sumter took place on April 12, 1861. With that, the American Civil War began. Hayes joined the Union army immediately. He promised to fight until the war was over. For the next four years, he would dedicate himself to the Union cause.

Hayes's regiment was first sent to western Virginia. Its job was to protect the Baltimore and Ohio Railroad from **rebel** raids. Army leaders knew that Hayes had been a successful lawyer before the war. In the summer of 1861, Major Hayes was ordered to leave his position and serve as a legal advisor to a Union general. When Hayes returned to his regiment in October, he received a promotion to the rank of lieutenant colonel. A promotion is a rise in rank or importance. The army gave Hayes the promotion to recognize his success.

The following spring, Hayes took command of nine **companies** of soldiers. One day, a much larger and more powerful Confederate force attacked without warning. Hayes displayed great skill and courage.

He swiftly moved his troops out of harm's way. The Union army recognized his skillful leadership. It offered Hayes another promotion to the rank of colonel, but he would have to leave his regiment. Hayes turned down the promotion. He chose to stay with his friends.

Next Hayes took part in the Battle of South Mountain on September 14, 1862. He was severely wounded in battle and had to be taken to a hospital. Hayes asked a messenger to send a telegram to Lucy, asking her to come at once. Unfortunately, the messenger forgot to include information about where Lucy could find her husband.

This photograph is a portrait of the officers of the 23rd Ohio Volunteer Regiment.

Lucy Hayes did what she could to help the Union army. She visited many camps and hospitals throughout the war to comfort soldiers. She earned the nickname "Mother Lucy" for her kindness.

Lucy and her brother, Dr. Joseph Webb, journeyed east to find Hayes, not knowing where to start. They spent six frantic days hunting for him in the hospitals of Baltimore and Washington. They continued until they finally found him in a hospital near Middletown, Maryland. Once Lucy was sure her husband was doing well, she wanted to help others. She made daily visits to comfort wounded and homesick soldiers.

After his recovery, Colonel Hayes took charge of his old regiment. Orders came for the troops to return to West Virginia. The winter passed quietly. In the spring and summer,

Hayes's troops took part in several raids to destroy Confederate supplies. They also helped stop the Southerners from communicating and traveling by railroad. Then Colonel Hayes learned of a Confederate plan to raid Union armies at several points on the other side of the Ohio River. He hired steamboats to carry his troops across the river. They succeeded in stopping raids in several locations. Then the 23rd Regiment returned to its post in Virginia.

Colonel Hayes played an important role in many other battles. In 1864, he took command of troops under General George Crook. He and Crook became close friends. For about two years, Hayes commanded his troops without receiving another promotion. Some of his friends brought this to the attention of General Crook and another officer, General Sheridan. The generals immediately promoted him to the rank of brigadier general. They recognized him for his bravery and effort in several battles. Then General Ulysses S. Grant, the head of the entire Union army, made Hayes a major general "for gallant and distinguished services during the campaigns of 1864 in West Virginia, and particularly in the battles of Fisher's Hill and Cedar Creek."

Finally, on April 3, 1865, the Union army captured the Confederate capital of Richmond. About 60,000 Union soldiers, led by General William Sherman, destroyed Southern railroads, factories, and plantations. They also destroyed any chance the South had of winning the war. General Robert E. Lee's Army of Northern Virginia **surrendered** on April 9. Soon other Confederate armies gave up as well, and the Civil War came to an end.

This photograph shows Confederate General Robert E. Lee (seated) just before he surrendered on April 9, 1865. Lee was from Virginia, and he fought for the South. Even so, he truly wanted to save the Union. His leadership and honesty earned him praise from both Southerners and Northerners.

HAYES DESCRIBED HIS FOUR YEARS in the Union army as "the best years of our lives. Those years were indeed golden." He considered the 10 months he served under the command of General Crook the most "golden" of all. Hayes was a brave and inspiring leader. He gave speeches that encouraged his troops. Crook was a man of action and decision. They made an excellent team. One example of their teamwork was the Battle of Fisher's Hill. General Sheridan planned to attack the enemy head on. But Crook realized that this was a dangerous plan. It might result in too many injuries and deaths among their soldiers. Crook created a plan that was less risky. He asked Hayes to use his fine speaking skills to convince General Sheridan to change his plan. General Sheridan finally agreed, and Crooks's plan worked. The Southern troops retreated. As Hayes put it, "They ran like sheep."

19

Chapter THREE

Political Life

With the war over, Hayes was happy to return to his family. But he would not return to his life in Ohio. While still in the army, he had been elected to the U.S. Congress.

IN THE FALL OF 1864, GENERAL HAYES WAS **nominated** as a **candidate** for the U.S. Congress. The war was not yet over. "I have other business just now," said Hayes. "Any man who would leave the army at this time … ought to be scalped." Hayes refused to **campaign,** but he won the election while he was still in the army. After the war, he served in Congress until 1867.

Hayes was a member of Congress during a difficult time in American history. With the Civil War over, there were angry debates in Congress and around the country about how to rebuild the South. Some people weren't sure the South should rejoin the Union at all. This period (from 1865 to 1877) is called **Reconstruction.** Congress wanted the South

20

After the war, much of the South was in ruins. People in every Southern state were starving. Many had lost their homes. The difficult process of rebuilding the war-torn South began shortly after General Lee surrendered.

Interesting Facts

▶ In elections after the Civil War, the Republican Party ran "bloody shirt" campaigns against the Southern Democrats. "Waving the bloody shirt" meant reminding voters that the **Democrats** had been responsible for the South's secession from the Union. Therefore, they deserved the blame for the bloody civil war. Republicans hoped this would help them win elections.

to be held responsible for the war. It also wanted to uphold the rights of the former slaves. But the South also desperately needed help. Cities and plantations were in ruins. Thousands of people were starving.

Andrew Johnson had taken office after President Lincoln was **assassinated** in April of 1865. Johnson was a Southerner, and he wanted to help other white Southerners. He especially wanted to help the common people who had lost so much during the war.

21

But Johnson seemed to pretend the war had never happened. He wanted to return life in the South to the way it had been before the war. He **pardoned** Confederate leaders, angering Northerners. He also did nothing to help the former slaves and supported the "black codes." These rules limited the rights of black Americans. The result was that their lives did not improve, even though slavery had been outlawed. Voters in the North rejected Johnson's plans. Congress decided to control Reconstruction. It sent **federal** troops to take charge of Southern capitals. Republican leaders also took over the local Southern governments.

Hayes did not take part in the bitter arguments in Congress about Reconstruction. Instead, he voted in agreement with other members of the Republican Party, most of whom wanted the North to take control of the South. Hayes made no public speeches during this time, and he was not well known to the public. Nevertheless, Ohio Republicans nominated him again in 1866.

This time, Hayes campaigned to win the election. He gave speeches about his goals. He said he supported the **amendments** to the **Constitution** that Congress had suggested. One amendment would give full rights to blacks as citizens of the United States. Another would guarantee black men the right to vote. (Women of all races could not vote until 1920.) Hayes also supported the Republican Party's plan to rebuild the war-torn South.

Hayes won the election. Then before he could return to Washington, he received a nomination to run for governor of Ohio. He decided to accept and gave up his seat in Congress. In 1867 and again in 1869, Hayes was elected governor. During his two **terms,** he proved to be a good leader. He earned the respect of Ohio's citizens. Governor Hayes took great interest in improving conditions in prisons and in mental hospitals. His interest in the

While Rutherford became more involved in state and national politics, Lucy's life still centered on their family. Many feminist groups hoped she would join the struggle for women's rights. After all, she had a college education, and that was an unusual achievement for women of the day. But Lucy did not get involved. She preferred to leave the business of politics to her husband.

hospitals was a personal one. His beloved sister, Fanny, suffered from mental illness. She had been hospitalized in the past.

Hayes ran for Congress again in 1872. He lost this election and decided to retire from politics. He returned to Fremont, the town where he had first practiced law and where his Uncle Sardis lived. A year later, Sardis Birchard died. Hayes inherited the great wealth that his successful uncle had earned over the years. This included his large, beautiful home called Spiegel Grove. Hayes and his family became leading citizens of Fremont.

The people of Ohio wanted Hayes to return to politics, so his retirement was brief. The Republican Party again nominated him as its candidate for governor in 1875. Later that year, he won the election and became the Ohio governor for a third time.

Hayes's popularity led to his nomination for president in 1876. In the November election, Hayes ran against a Democrat, Samuel Tilden. At first, it seemed that Tilden had won the election. But some people believed his supporters had cheated. Votes from three Southern states—Florida, South Carolina, and

Louisiana—were in doubt. Democrats from those states claimed that Tilden had won. Republican voters refused to accept the Democratic victory. They claimed that the votes actually had gone to Hayes and said the Democrats had cheated. No one knew for sure who had really won.

Government leaders discussed the problem for many weeks. The year ended with no decision about who would become the next president. A special **election commission** had to decide which candidate, Hayes or Tilden, had won.

Hayes's Uncle Sardis left him a beautiful mansion, called Spiegel Grove, in the town of Fremont. Lucy and Rutherford posed for this portrait at the home.

25

Samuel Tilden ran against Hayes in the presidential election of 1876. No one knew for sure who had won, so an election commission had to decide who would become president.

To the Friends of
TILDEN AND REFORM!
HONEST SAM. TILDEN,

CAMPAIGN SONG AND CHORUS

BANNER OF TILDEN & HENDRICKS.

TILDEN & HENDRICKS REFORM MARCH.

CINCINNATI, JOHN CHURCH & CO.

CHICAGO, ROOT & SONS MUSIC CO.

The Southern Democrats finally agreed to accept Mr. Hayes if he would remove federal troops from the South. Hayes and the Republicans agreed. On March 2, 1877, Hayes won the election by only one vote of the election commission.

AFTER THE CIVIL WAR WAS over, the Northern states wanted to keep former Confederate leaders out of U.S. politics. They also wanted to be sure the South would remain loyal to the Union. Congress passed the Reconstruction Acts to make sure Southerners would not cause problems in the future. These acts allowed the federal government to send military forces to the South. They also allowed Northerners to set up and control new Southern governments.

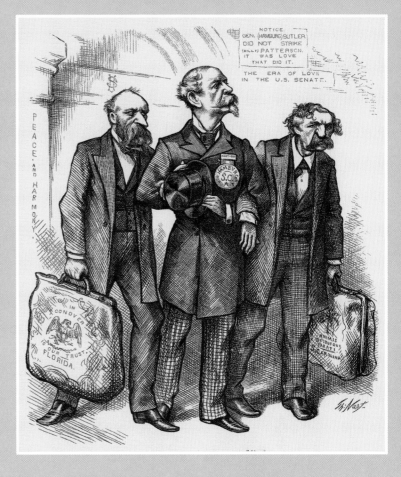

Northerners who traveled to the South during Reconstruction were called **carpetbaggers.** They got this name because many carried their belongings in bags made from carpeting. Most of these Northerners were educated people, such as teachers, businessmen, and former soldiers. They wanted to help restore the schools, farms, and businesses that were destroyed during the war. Unfortunately, a few dishonest people went there to make money from the misfortunes of the Southerners. The greedy actions of these individuals, many of whom were politicians, gave all the carpetbaggers a bad name.

Chapter FOUR

A Leader for All

When Hayes became president, Democrats vowed to make his term as difficult as possible. They believed he had won the election unfairly, so they would not help him achieve his goals.

RUTHERFORD B. HAYES WAS A GOOD PRESIDENT, and historians usually say that he was an honest man. Some call him a "gentleman of politics." Still, his victory over Samuel Tilden created some doubt about his honesty. This often made his presidency difficult.

Because of the problems during the election, Hayes took the oath of office in a private ceremony at the White House. He became the 19th president of the United States on March 4, 1877. William A. Wheeler of New York served as his vice president. Congress and the political parties usually had more power than the president at this time in U.S. history. Republican members of Congress expected to control Hayes, just as they had controlled the two presidents before him. Hayes would not let this happen. He gave a speech at his **inauguration** that told people what he believed. "He serves his party best who serves his country best," said Hayes. This meant that he planned to do what was best for the American people. He would do it even if it meant disagreeing with other Republicans.

Hayes's enemies still believed he had won the election through fraud, or a dishonest act. They even nick-named him "Rutherfraud." Hayes didn't let his opponents bother him. He believed he deserved to be the president and that he had won the election fairly. Hayes forged ahead, doing what he believed was right for the country. By the end of his term, his honesty, fairness, and independence won respect.

As Hayes had promised, troops were removed from the South. When the troops left, the governments set up by Northerners collapsed. Soon, Southerners had control of

There were many new inventions around the time that President Hayes was in office. One of these was Thomas Edison's phonograph, which later became known as the record player. Edison is shown here with his invention. Hayes requested that he demonstrate it at the White House.

their state governments again. The long, bitter Reconstruction was over.

President Hayes is remembered most as the president who ended Reconstruction. But he dealt with many other important issues of the day. For one thing, he tried to stop corruption in the government. Corruption is dishonesty, especially when people accomplish a goal by doing something wrong. Politicians often gave important, high-paying government positions to people who shared their ideas and who helped get them elected. These people weren't always the best choice for the jobs. Hayes believed that this was dishonest. He believed that government jobs should not be used to reward people.

To fight this corruption, Hayes ordered that no federal government employee could take part in political activities, such as election campaigns. This angered many members of Congress. Hayes would not listen to their complaints. Whenever he could, he gave government positions to the best-qualified people.

Hayes always did what he thought was right, even if it challenged the views of powerful, wealthy Americans. He believed

30

big businesses often took advantage of their employees. He tried to help poor and **working-class** Americans. "The vast wealth and power is in the hands of the few," said Hayes. He wanted more Americans to enjoy the nation's good fortune.

Some of President Hayes's ideas were very modern for his time. He took an interest in helping immigrants, people who came to live in America from other countries. He signed a **bill** that allowed the first women lawyers to appear before the U.S. **Supreme Court,** the most powerful court in the nation. He also was the first president to talk about protecting the environment.

Perhaps most important, Hayes made good decisions about how to manage the government's money. This helped make the nation stronger. Following an idea of President Ulysses S. Grant, Hayes returned the nation's money system to the **gold standard.** This meant that the government had to have enough gold to back every U.S. dollar that was printed. During the Civil War, the government printed more money than usual to help pay for the war. U.S. dollars were

For years, Chinese immigrants had traveled to California to find work. They took the most difficult jobs, ones that no one else wanted. When jobs became scarce, other immigrants attacked the Chinese, thinking they were taking all the jobs. Congress tried to solve the problem by stopping the Chinese from coming to America. Hayes believed this bill was unfair. He worked to limit immigration in a way that he felt was right.

worth less than before because there wasn't enough gold for each dollar. Hayes made sure this policy came to an end.

When Hayes entered office, he promised not to run for a second term as president.

Always a man of his word, he kept this promise. By the time his first term was over, Americans respected his leadership. When people asked him to run for another term, he refused. The president told the public that he had no "fondness for political life."

Hayes retired to his home in Fremont, Ohio. From his front porch, he delivered a short speech about what he thought a retired president should do with his life. "Let him, like every other good American citizen," said Hayes, "be willing and prompt to bear his

Lucy and Rutherford returned to their lovely home in Ohio after his presidency. They were happy to be among family and friends again.

part in every useful work that will promote the welfare and the happiness of his family, his town, his state, and his country."

Hayes continued to help people. He worked to improve the conditions in prisons. He made sure that soldiers who had fought in the Civil War received the retirement money the government had promised them. He fought to make sure that every American —including blacks and Native Americans— could have an education. Lucy stayed busy, too. She taught Sunday school and helped organize suppers and festivals for her church. She spent as much time as possible with her children and grandchildren.

Rutherford and Lucy Hayes lived out the rest of their lives at Spiegel Grove in Fremont. In 1889, Lucy collapsed while watching a tennis match and soon died. Three and a half years later, shortly after he visited Lucy's grave, Rutherford died on January 17, 1893. He was 70 years old. "I know that I am going where Lucy is," Hayes told his doctor, shortly before he passed away. "I am not unhappy, my life is an exceptionally happy one."

34

PRESIDENT AND MRS. HAYES HAD THREE OF THEIR FIVE CHILDREN LIVING with them at the White House: Webb, Fanny, and Scott. Webb had graduated from Cornell University and became his father's secretary.

This picture was taken in the White House conservatory, where plants and flowers were grown. Scott is shown at Lucy's left, and Fanny is to her right. The other child is a friend of the family. While in the White House, setting a good example for the American people was important to the Hayes family. They started every day by reading a chapter from the Bible. Each member of the family read a verse. Then they all said the Lord's Prayer together. In the evening, they sang hymns and again said their prayers. Each Sunday morning, the President and Mrs. Hayes walked to the nearby Foundry Methodist Church to worship. Dancing and card parties were not allowed during the family's stay at the White House. Many dinner guests expected to enjoy wine with their meals, but the Hayeses never served alcoholic drinks. For this, Mrs. Hayes was nicknamed "Lemonade Lucy."

1817 Rutherford's parents move from Vermont to Delaware, Ohio. Mr. Hayes buys a business and rents farmland. The family builds the first brick house in town.

1822 Rutherford's father dies in late summer. Rutherford B. Hayes is born on October 4.

1836 Hayes's Uncle Sardis sends him to private school to prepare for college.

1842 Hayes graduates from Kenyon College at the head of his class.

1845 Hayes receives a law degree from Harvard University. He starts his law career in Lower Sandusky, Ohio (later called Fremont).

1847 Hayes first meets Lucy Webb.

1849 Hayes moves to Cincinnati and becomes a successful lawyer. He becomes a member of the Republican Party, in part because the party opposes slavery.

1852 Rutherford Hayes and Lucy Webb marry in December.

1853 Hayes begins to defend runaway slaves in court. The Hayes's first child, Sardis, is born in November.

1861 The Civil War begins on April 12 when the South fires on Fort Sumter. Hayes joins the 23rd Ohio Volunteer Regiment.

His regiment travels to Virginia to protect railroads from rebel attacks. During the summer, he provides legal council to a Union general.

1862 Hayes takes part in the Battle of South Mountain on September 14. He is severely wounded and must be taken to the hospital. Lucy Hayes travels east to care for her husband. She also visits other wounded soldiers, earning devotion and respect from the troops.

1864 Hayes is promoted to major general by General Ulysses S. Grant. General Hayes is nominated to run for Congress. He refuses to leave his military duties to campaign but is still elected by a large majority.

1865 General Robert E. Lee's Army of Northern Virginia surrenders on April 9. Other Confederate armies soon give up as well, and the Civil War comes to an end. Hayes takes his seat in Congress. The period known as the Reconstruction begins, during which the nation helps to rebuild the South and accepts it back into the Union.

1866 Hayes is reelected to Congress.

1867 Before Hayes returns to Congress, he is nominated to run for governor of Ohio. He wins the election.

1869 Hayes is elected for a second term as the governor of Ohio.

1872 Hayes runs for Congress again. He loses the election and decides to retire from politics. He and his family return to Fremont, the town where he first practiced law and where his Uncle Sardis lives.

1873 Sardis Birchard dies. Hayes inherits his uncle's wealth and the home he built in Fremont.

1875 Hayes is reelected the governor of Ohio.

1876 Governor Hayes is nominated as the Republican Party candidate for the presidency. His opponent, Democrat Samuel Tilden, wins the popular vote. Republicans accuse the Democrats of fraud, so Tilden does not take office. Congress must decide whether Hayes or Tilden will become the president. It selects a special electoral commission to make the decision.

1877 On March 2, the electoral commission elects Rutherford Hayes as the 19th U.S. president after he promises Southern Democrats that he will withdraw federal troops from the South. On March 4, he is sworn into office. As promised, Hayes removes federal troops from the South. This act ends Reconstruction. He also attempts to stop the practice of giving important government jobs to the friends of politicians. He issues an order that stops people with government jobs from taking part in political activities.

1878 Hayes begins to deal with problems in the U.S. monetary system. He returns the nation to the gold standard.

1879 President Hayes continues to fight corruption in the government. He fires future president Chester A. Arthur and future governor of New York Alonzo B. Cornell. In February, President Hayes approves a bill allowing women to practice law before the Supreme Court.

1880 Hayes refuses to sign a bill that he feels is prejudiced against Chinese immigrants. Hayes announces that he will not seek a second term.

1881 President Hayes's term of office is over. He retires to his home in Fremont, Ohio, where he continues to help the poor and minorities. He also works to make it possible for all Americans to get an education.

1889 Lucy Hayes suffers a stroke and dies.

1893 Rutherford B. Hayes dies on January 17 at age 70.

37

amendments (uh-MEND-mentz)
Amendments are changes or additions made to the U.S. Constitution or other documents. Hayes supported amendments that helped former slaves.

assassinate (uh-SASS-ih-nayt)
To assassinate means to murder someone, especially a well-known person. Andrew Johnson took office after President Lincoln was assassinated.

bill (BILL)
A bill is an idea for a new law that is presented to a group of lawmakers. Hayes refused to sign a bill that was prejudiced against Chinese immigrants.

campaign (kam-PAYN)
A campaign is the process of running for an election, including activities such as giving speeches or attending rallies. Hayes won his first election to Congress even though he did not campaign.

candidate (KAN-dih-det)
A candidate is a person running in an election. The Republican Party nominated Hayes as its presidential candidate in 1876.

carpetbaggers (KAR-pet-bag-erz)
Carpetbaggers were Northerners who traveled to the Southern states after the Civil War. Carpetbaggers were often disliked because some came to make money from the misfortunes of Southerners.

civil war (SIV-il WAR)
A civil war is a war between opposing groups of citizens within the same country. The American Civil War began after the South seceded from the Union.

companies (KUM-puh-neez)
Companies are parts of an army that are commanded by a captain. Hayes took command of nine companies of soldiers in 1862.

Confederate (kun-FED-uh-ret)
Confederate refers to the slave states (or the people who lived in those states) that left the Union in 1860 and 1861. The people of the South were called Confederates.

constitution (kon-stih-TOO-shun)
A constitution is the set of basic principles that govern a state, country, or society. The U.S. Constitution defines the principles that govern the United States.

Democrats (DEM-uh-kratz)
Democrats are members of the Democratic Party. The Democratic Party is one of the two major political parties in the United States.

distinguished (dis-TING-gwisht)
If people are distinguished, they stand out for their excellence or achievements. Hayes hoped to be distinguished for his good character.

election commission (ee-LEK-shun kuh-MISH-un)
The election commission was a group of 10 congressmen and five Supreme Court justices formed to choose the president after problems arose in the election of 1876. The election commission decided that Hayes would be the next president.

federal (FED-ur-ul)
Federal means having to do with the central government of the United States, rather than a state or city government. After the Civil War, the United States government sent federal troops to keep control of Southern capitals.

gold standard (GOLD STAN-durd)
The gold standard is a money system that gives paper money and coins their value. During Hayes's term, every U.S. dollar was worth a certain amount of gold, and the government had to have enough gold to back every dollar.

inauguration (ih-nawg-yuh-RAY-shun)
An inauguration is the ceremony that takes place when a new president begins his term. President Hayes's inauguration was the first to take place at the White House.

inherit (in-HAIR-it)
If people inherit something, it is given to them when someone else dies. Hayes inherited Spiegel Grove from his Uncle Sardis.

nominate (NOM-ih-nayt)
If a political party nominates someone, they choose him or her to run for a political office. Hayes was nominated as a candidate for the U.S. Congress while he was still in the army.

pardon (PAR-den)
If a leader pardons people, he or she excuses them for their crimes or misdeeds. President Johnson pardoned many Confederates.

perseverance (pur-seh-VEER-intz)
Perseverance means never giving up when you have set out to achieve something. Young Rutherford wanted to be known for his perseverance.

**political parties
(puh-LIT-uh-kul PAR-teez)**
Political parties are groups of people who share similar ideas about how to run a government. Hayes was a member of the Republican political party.

politics (PAWL-ih-tiks)
Politics refers to the actions and practices of the government. Hayes first became active in politics when he lived in Cincinnati.

rebel (REB-ul)
A rebel is a person who does not obey the laws of his or her country. The Confederate rebels wanted to leave the Union and form their own country.

**Reconstruction
(ree-kun-STRUK-shun)**
Reconstruction (1865-1877) was the period in U.S. history following the Civil War. During this time, the Southern states were accepted back into the Union, but there were many disagreements about how to do this.

regiment (REJ-eh-ment)
A regiment is a group of soldiers led by a colonel. In June of 1861, Hayes became a major of the 23rd Ohio Volunteer Regiment.

**Republican Party
(re-PUB-lih-ken PAR-tee)**
The Republican Party is one of the two major political parties in the United States. Rutherford Hayes was a member of the Republican Party.

secede (suh-SEED)
If a group secedes, it separates from a larger group. The Southern states seceded from the Union in 1860 and 1861 to form their own country.

Supreme Court
(suh-PREEM KORT)
The Supreme Court is the highest court in the United States, which means it is more powerful than all other American courts. Hayes signed a bill that allowed the first women lawyers to appear before the U.S. Supreme Court.

surrender (suh-REN-dur)
If an army surrenders, it gives up to its enemy. General Robert E. Lee's Army of Northern Virginia surrendered on April 9, 1865.

terms (TERMZ)
Terms are the length of time politicians can keep their positions by law. A U.S. president's term of office is four years.

union (YOON-yen)
A union is the joining together of two people or groups of people, such as states. The Union is another name for the United States.

working class (WER-king KLASS)
The working class is made up of people who work for wages. It especially means people who do manual labor, such as construction or manufacturing jobs.

President	Birthplace	Life Span	Presidency	Political Party	First Lady
George Washington	Virginia	1732–1799	1789–1797	None	Martha Dandridge Custis Washington
John Adams	Massachusetts	1735–1826	1797–1801	Federalist	Abigail Smith Adams
Thomas Jefferson	Virginia	1743–1826	1801–1809	Democratic-Republican	widower
James Madison	Virginia	1751–1836	1809–1817	Democratic Republican	Dolley Payne Todd Madison
James Monroe	Virginia	1758–1831	1817–1825	Democratic Republican	Elizabeth Kortright Monroe
John Quincy Adams	Massachusetts	1767–1848	1825–1829	Democratic-Republican	Louisa Johnson Adams
Andrew Jackson	South Carolina	1767–1845	1829–1837	Democrat	widower
Martin Van Buren	New York	1782–1862	1837–1841	Democrat	widower
William H. Harrison	Virginia	1773–1841	1841	Whig	Anna Symmes Harrison
John Tyler	Virginia	1790–1862	1841–1845	Whig	Letitia Christian Tyler / Julia Gardiner Tyler
James K. Polk	North Carolina	1795–1849	1845–1849	Democrat	Sarah Childress Polk

Our PRESIDENTS

President	Birthplace	Life Span	Presidency	Political Party	First Lady
Zachary Taylor	Virginia	1784–1850	1849–1850	Whig	Margaret Mackall Smith Taylor
Millard Fillmore	New York	1800–1874	1850–1853	Whig	Abigail Powers Fillmore
Franklin Pierce	New Hampshire	1804–1869	1853–1857	Democrat	Jane Means Appleton Pierce
James Buchanan	Pennsylvania	1791–1868	1857–1861	Democrat	never married
Abraham Lincoln	Kentucky	1809–1865	1861–1865	Republican	Mary Todd Lincoln
Andrew Johnson	North Carolina	1808–1875	1865–1869	Democrat	Eliza McCardle Johnson
Ulysses S. Grant	Ohio	1822–1885	1869–1877	Republican	Julia Dent Grant
Rutherford B. Hayes	Ohio	1822–1893	1877–1881	Republican	Lucy Webb Hayes
James A. Garfield	Ohio	1831–1881	1881	Republican	Lucretia Rudolph Garfield
Chester A. Arthur	Vermont	1829–1886	1881–1885	Republican	widower
Grover Cleveland	New Jersey	1837–1908	1885–1889	Democrat	Frances Folsom Cleveland

Our PRESIDENTS

President	Birthplace	Life Span	Presidency	Political Party	First Lady
Benjamin Harrison	Ohio	1833–1901	1889–1893	Republican	Caroline Scott Harrison
Grover Cleveland	New Jersey	1837–1908	1893–1897	Democrat	Frances Folsom Cleveland
William McKinley	Ohio	1843–1901	1897–1901	Republican	Ida Saxton McKinley
Theodore Roosevelt	New York	1858–1919	1901–1909	Republican	Edith Kermit Carow Roosevelt
William H. Taft	Ohio	1857–1930	1909–1913	Republican	Helen Herron Taft
Woodrow Wilson	Virginia	1856–1924	1913–1921	Democrat	Ellen L. Axson Wilson Edith Bolling Galt Wilson
Warren G. Harding	Ohio	1865–1923	1921–1923	Republican	Florence Kling De Wolfe Harding
Calvin Coolidge	Vermont	1872–1933	1923–1929	Republican	Grace Goodhue Coolidge
Herbert C. Hoover	Iowa	1874–1964	1929–1933	Republican	Lou Henry Hoover
Franklin D. Roosevelt	New York	1882–1945	1933–1945	Democrat	Anna Eleanor Roosevelt Roosevelt
Harry S. Truman	Missouri	1884–1972	1945–1953	Democrat	Elizabeth Wallace Truman

President	Birthplace	Life Span	Presidency	Political Party	First Lady
Dwight D. Eisenhower	Texas	1890–1969	1953–1961	Republican	Mary "Mamie" Doud Eisenhower
John F. Kennedy	Massachusetts	1917–1963	1961–1963	Democrat	Jacqueline Bouvier Kennedy
Lyndon B. Johnson	Texas	1908–1973	1963–1969	Democrat	Claudia Alta Taylor Johnson
Richard M. Nixon	California	1913–1994	1969–1974	Republican	Thelma Catherine Ryan Nixon
Gerald Ford	Nebraska	1913–	1974–1977	Republican	Elizabeth "Betty" Bloomer Warren Ford
James Carter	Georgia	1924–	1977–1981	Democrat	Rosalynn Smith Carter
Ronald Reagan	Illinois	1911–	1981–1989	Republican	Nancy Davis Reagan
George Bush	Massachusetts	1924–	1989–1993	Republican	Barbara Pierce Bush
William Clinton	Arkansas	1946–	1993–2001	Democrat	Hillary Rodham Clinton
George W. Bush	Connecticut	1946–	2001–	Republican	Laura Welch Bush

Qualifications

To run for president, a candidate must

- be at least 35 years old
- be a citizen who was born in the United States
- have lived in the United States for 14 years

Term of Office

A president's term of office is four years. No president can stay in office for more than two terms.

Election Date

The presidential election takes place every four years on the first Tuesday of November.

Inauguration Date

Presidents are inaugurated on January 20.

Oath of Office

I do solemnly swear I will faithfully execute the office of the President of the United States and will to the best of my ability preserve, protect, and defend the Constitution of the United States.

Write a Letter to the President

One of the best things about being a U.S. citizen is that Americans get to participate in their government. They can speak out if they feel government leaders aren't doing their jobs. They can also praise leaders who are going the extra mile. Do you have something you'd like the president to do? Should the president worry more about the environment and encourage people to recycle? Should the government spend more money on our schools? You can write a letter to the president to say how you feel!

1600 Pennsylvania Avenue
Washington, D.C. 20500

You can even send an e-mail to: president@whitehouse.gov

For Further INFORMATION

Internet Sites

Visit the Rutherford B. Hayes Library and Museum, located at his home in Fremont:
http://www.rbhayes.org

Learn more about Rutherford B. Hayes during the civil war:
http://americancivilwar.com/hayes.html

Learn more about the Reconstruction era:
www.historychannel.com

Learn more about all the presidents and visit the White House:
http://www.whitehouse.gov/WH/glimpse/presidents/html/presidents.html
http://www.thepresidency.org/presinfo.htm
http://www.americanpresidents.org/

Books

Murphy, Jim. *The Boys' War: Confederate and Union Soldiers Talk About the Civil War.* New York: Clarion, 1990.

Ray, Delia. *A Nation Torn: The Story of How the Civil War Began.* New York: Puffin, 1996.

Hansen, Joyce. *Bury Me Not in a Land of Slaves: African-Americans in the Time of Reconstruction (Social Studies, Cultures and People).* New York: Franklin Watts, 2000.

Nadine, Corinne J. and Rose Blue. *Civil War Ends. Assassination, Reconstruction, and the Aftermath.* Austin, TX: Raintree Steck-Vaughn, 1999.

Schleichert, Elizabeth. *The Thirteenth Amendment: Ending Slavery.* Springfield, NJ: Enslow Publishers, 1998.

Anthony, Carl Sferrazza. *America's Most Influential First Ladies.* Minneapolis, MN: Oliver Press, 1992.

Gormley, Beatrice. *First Ladies: Women Who Called the White House Home.* New York: Scholastic, 1997.